AF624680

Towards The Sun

A journey of healing.

Nancy Cowan

BookLeaf Publishing
India | USA | UK

Made with ❤ on the BookLeaf Publishing Platform
www.bookleafpub.in
www.bookleafpub.com

Dedication

For all the people who’ve inspired, supported and loved me in the darkness.

Preface

My last book was my story of what happened.
This book tracks the imprint of the trauma I experienced and how, years later, it came to haunt me.
I felt like I had to speed along the healing process, being told to just get over it or to seek closure, to look forward at all the good things that have happened since.
However without looking the personal affects of the trauma in the eye I felt like I was stuck in a place of healing like it had stopped and I couldn't put my finger on what it was. Following many conversations with family, friends and my counsellor I am beginning to sort through the stuff I had pushed into the cupboard because the cupboard began to overflow, things kept falling out and I was always tripping over them.
This has not been an easy journey for my family either and I am very thankful that they stand steadfast beside me.

Acknowledgements

To everyone who helped make this possible.

1. Why Now?

It's been years but the questions still come.
Why now?
Why is the ache returning when I thought I had buried it?
My days were long and soft, peaceful,
But then a sound, a smell, a picture, an event pulls it all apart.
And suddenly I'm back there.
Why now?
Why does it feel like the past has followed me through time like a shadow that refuses to die?
I thought I had earned rest, earned the right to move on,
But here it is again creeping under my skin.
My body remembers even when my mind tries to forget.
It remembers the tightness in my chest.
The moments I thought I'd outrun,
But they've been waiting.
Shut up in a cupboard but now spilling out.
Why now?
The question hangs like fog clouding my thoughts,

But in its weight there is something else,
A quiet understanding that healing isn't linear,
That wounds don't close until the right moment,
Until the soul has gathered enough strength to look them in the eye.
It's not about time but about the courage to face what's left behind.
To let the scars speak,
To let the heart break through the pain.
And maybe the healing I seek is waiting in the question itself...
Why now?
Because now, I am ready.

2. Tangled

Healing is a tangled thread,
Dancing across the night sky.
Each thread a frustration,
Resisting the pull of careful hands.
Unravelling what the heart is willing to let go.
Each thread reveals,
A quiet passage through,
A galaxy of revelations.

3. Guilt

Grasping at the thought of what you endured,
Underneath my love is a heavy regret.
I see your eyes, carrying pain you didn't deserve,
Love couldn't shield you from the storms he brought.
Time cannot erase, but I hope it can mend us.

4. Know your Worth

I stood in front of the mirror,
the glass cold,
reflecting a face I barely recognised.
Shame whispered softly,
filling the silence with its heavy weight,
Doubt curling around my thoughts like smoke I couldn't escape.
But then,
Slowly,
I started to write, with shaking hands—
Uncertain words on my mirror,
Faint echoes of something I had forgotten:
"Know your worth."
It felt strange at first,
Unbelievable.
But with each repetition,
Small cracks in the armour that had kept me from myself appeared.
The reflection didn't change,
Not at first,

but in the way I looked,
The way I saw,
A shift began to settle.
And in that light,
I began to soften,
The harsh edges of self-criticism slowly melting away.
It wasn't sudden, this journey of seeing, believing and becoming,
But one day,
I stood before the mirror again,
and for the first time,
I saw myself;
Without question,
Without shame,
Just as I am.
And I understood and knew my worth.

5. Undeserving : Deserving

How do you know you're deserving?

-It's not about the weight of my wounds,
but in how I rise, in what I choose to seek after the fall.

But doesn't the pain mean you're undeserving?

- No. Pain is only a part of the story,
not the whole of me. When the storm clears,
I search for the light breaking through the cracks.

What if the light doesn't come?

-Then I'll keep moving, even through shadows.
Each step forward whispers, 'I am still deserving.'

And that's true?

-Yes. Being deserving isn't tied to what hurt me.
It's in every choice I make to reach for something better.

Healing isn't about proving anything.
It's in the seeking, the trying.
It is the hope that grows in the soil of my survival.

6. Patience

Patience is a heavy cloak,
wrapped tight around my shoulders,
demanding stillness,
asking me to sit with the ache.

Frustration tugs at my edges,
sharp and impatient,
wanting to break free,
but patience holds,
soft, yet firm,
whispering:
"Stay, just a little longer."

Healing moves in whispers,
in the long pauses between breaths,
and in those quiet moments,
patience is the only strength
that carries me through.

7. Butterfly

In shadows, my soul folds inward,
A chrysalis forms, holding silence and pain.
Traumatic memories wrap tightly around me,
Like a leaf curling under frost.

Inside, my work is slow,
Time stitching strength into fragile threads.
Dreams begin to unfurl,
Seeking shape in the stillness.

When the chrysalis opens,
Wings of healing emerge, delicate but steady.
A butterfly rises,
Its flight shaped by struggle.

Healing is this—
Transformation. Rising.
Lifting me toward the light.

8. Some Days are Easier than Others

The road to healing winds and shifts like a rollercoaster.
Some days are easier than others— the climb feels light,
the air clear.
Other days, the weight pulls me down and I struggle to
keep my footing.
But I remind myself to be gentle, to breathe, to give
space to the ache.
Knowing that some steps will be slo and that's okay.
I can't rush this journey but I can be patient with myself.
Each day, even the hard ones, is part of the process.
I am learning to trust it.
One step at a time.

9. Hope

Stars pierce night's veil,
Guiding my heart through the dark -
Hope shines quietly.

10. The Story of the Unsung Hero

There was this distance,
Between who I was and who I am now.
Yet still my pulse raced without reason.
Still the weight of the shadow clung to my back,
Even when the sun was bright.
There was this quiet war,
In the spaces between my thoughts.
So quiet, no one could hear,
But some could see.
I thought that my fight was over,
But the battle never seemed to end.
I learned to carry the burden,
Not by choice, but by necessity,
And in the silence, I found my strength.
I was not a hero through triumph,
But through endurance,
Through the simple act of surviving
When everything else seemed to fall apart.
Now I stand, still bruised,

But no longer broken.
The struggle is not finished,
But it no longer owns me.
I carry the weight,
But it no longer defines me.
I've learned that strength isn't loud,
It's the quiet persistence of continuing,
Even when the world can't see the fight.

11. Accepting Help

I turn from their hands,
afraid of what I might need—
solitude feels safe.
But their love breaks through the dark,
showing me the strength to heal.

12. You love my darkness

You see me—a forest at midnight,
my branches clawing at the stars,
my roots tangled with serpents
that hiss their warnings to the world.

But you do not flinch.
You walk deeper,
as if my shadows were lanterns
guiding you home.

I warned you of the snakes,
the way they coil like whispers
around my thoughts,
venom dripping in the cracks of my smiles.

But you only smiled back,
your love like an antidote
that dared the poison to strike.

I am the sea in a storm,

wild and unyielding,
my depths holding broken ships
and the screams of sailors lost to time.

Yet you wade in,
arms wide as if inviting the tide,
telling me my wreckage
is nothing to fear.

You love my darkness
like the moon loves the night,
casting your light across every shadow
without trying to banish it.

You see my chaos
not as a thing to tame
but as the song you've always known,
the melody that makes you whole.

Even the snakes, those writhing fears I call my own,
seem to bow to your presence,
their venom turned to quiet ink
as you write your love across me.

You stay,
not because I am safe,

but because I am real,
and you would not have me any other way.

13. Leaving Survival Mode

I did not know
how to let go of survival—
it clung to me
like a shadow at twilight,
but as I stepped into the light,
it began to fade,
whispering goodbye
as I breathed in the air
I once thought would crush me.

14. Déjà Vu

I've been here before,
In this moment,
In this breath,
As if time loops back on itself,
Like a faded photograph,
A memory with edges blurred.
The air feels too familiar,
The words on your lips
Sound like something I've heard,
But from where?
From when?
I can't place it—
Yet it tugs at me,
Like the echo of a dream
I forgot upon waking.
I watch myself,
Living a life I thought was new,
A part of me remembers,
But refuses to fully know.
The seconds stretch,

Like the pause before a song,
A fleeting recognition
That slips through my fingers
The moment I reach for it.
It's not quite déjà vu,
Not a return,
But a crossing—
A moment split,
A thread connecting past and present,
That frays just before I grasp it,
Leaving only the quiet hum
Of something unfinished,
But always known.

15. Towards the Sun

Once, I was a seed buried deep,
pressed beneath the weight of my pain,
but now I stretch,
my roots drinking the rain of forgiveness,
my leaves unfurling
towards the sun of my own light.

Healing is not a straight road,
but a spiral staircase,
each step higher
but circling the shadows I left below.

The wounds once raw,
red as a sunset's edge,
are now gold veins through the marble of my skin,
proof that I was broken
but refused to stay shattered.

Towards the sun,
I tilt my face,

no longer afraid of its brilliance,
no longer hiding in the shade of doubt.
I have learned to shine with it,
a mirror reflecting its glow
back into the world.

Healing is the flight of a bird
that has shed its broken wing,
soaring into skies
that no longer hold storms,
but promise horizons
only I can reach.

16. Rainbow

Through the darkest clouds,
a rainbow bends, soft and bright—
peace grows from the dust.

17. Apology

I owe myself an apology,
for the times I ignored my pain,
for letting myself carry burdens
I never should have borne.
I'm sorry for the silence I forced,
for believing brokenness was something to endure,
for thinking love could thrive in chains.
I see myself now—strong, worthy,
beautiful in my scars.
I will no longer shrink,
will no longer dismiss my needs.
No more smoke, no more mirrors.
I was always enough.

18. Penny

You don't have to speak—
I feel the ache in your silence,
sense the weight you carry
in the slump of your shoulders.
I sit beside you,
quiet and steadfast,
my head resting near your hand,
a small anchor pulling you back.
I don't need the words
you can't find,
only to stay by your side—
steady, patient, here.
My love is endless,
without question or pause.
I see your struggle
and offer all I have:
A gentle nudge when tears fall,
my warmth against the cold world,
a reminder that healing

can begin with me—
your steady light.

19. Imprint

It's not about the details,
the names, the dates, the places—
not about reliving the moments,
but understanding the imprint they left.
It isn't about recounting
the past over and over,
but understanding how it shaped me—
how it left its mark in my body,
my mind, my spirit.

It's in the way my hands shake
when I feel threatened,
the rash that spreads when I'm overwhelmed,
the way my breath catches
in the quiet of a trigger.
It's in the nightmares that still visit,
even when the night is calm,
the sudden rush of fear
when nothing is actually wrong.

Healing isn't about going over the past,
but feeling the weight of it—
how it lingers in my body,
in the tension I hold without knowing.
It's about learning to breathe again,
to trust that my body can be safe,
to understand the reactions that I've carried
as echoes of what once was,
instead of being defined by them.

I don't need to remember everything,
but I need to feel where the imprint lies—
to recognize how it still moves through me—
how it lives in the places I can't see.
the tremors, the shadows,
and find a way to move through them,
and slowly, finding peace in the quiet spaces between.

20. Apricity

The winter sun rests gently on my skin,
its warmth a quiet promise,
soft as a whisper,
breaking through the ice that once
froze my soul.
But apricity arrives,
its golden fingers brushing the ice,
coaxing me to thaw.
Trauma was the winter of my soul,
long nights heavy with silence,
days muted in gray.
I forgot what it meant to feel warmth,
to believe the sun could touch me
without burning.
But here it is now,
a gentle, forgiving light,
not demanding my bloom,
only offering its presence,
as steady as breath.
The warmth feels unfamiliar—

like kindness long absent,
But I turn my face to it,
hesitant, yet it cradles me,
as if I had never been cold.
Overcoming is not a firestorm,
not a sudden blaze;
it is apricity—
a patient, persistent warmth
melting the frost of old wounds.
The sun does not rush me.
It waits as I unfold,
slow as winter's end,
but certain as spring.

www.ingramcontent.com/pod-product-compliance
Lightning Source LLC
Chambersburg PA
CBHW051749130826
49812CB00033B/1066
* 9 7 8 9 3 6 7 3 9 9 7 8 1 *